Albert Tapper & Peter Press

A Guy Goes Into a Bar...

MJF BOOKS

NEW YORK

Published by MJF Books
Fine Communications
Two Lincoln Square
60 West 66th Street
New York, NY 10023

A Guy Goes Into a Bar...
LC Control Number 00-136512
ISBN 1-56731-418-X

Manufactured in the United States of America on acid-free paper

MJF Books and the MJF colophon are trademarks of Fine Creative Media,
Inc.

10   9   8   7   6   5   4   3   2

A guy goes into a bar, sits down, and orders a drink. He starts eating the beer nuts at the bar and he hears a voice say, "Wow! You look *great* tonight!"

The man looks over at the bartender, who seems to ignore the voice. The man keeps drinking and eating beer nuts until he hears something again!

"That's an awesome shirt! You are amazing."

He looks around and he's the only guy in the place, so he asks the bartender if he had heard anything and the bartender asks, "Was the voice saying bad things or good things?" The man replies, "Good things, why?"

The bartender says, "It must be the complimentary nuts."

A Guy Goes Into A Bar

A guy goes into a bar, obviously very drunk, and says to the bartender, "I'd like to buy everyone in the bar a drink, and get one for yourself, too!"

The bartender makes the drinks and everyone raises their glasses and yells *"Cheers!"* and down their drinks.

The bartender says, "That'll be $37.50." The drunk says, "Kiss my big butt, 'cuz I don't have any money!"

This infuriates the bartender, who then jumps over the bar and beats the living hell out of the drunk and throws him out into the street.

The next day the same drunk walks into the same bar and says, "I'd like to buy the whole bar a drink, and get one for yourself, too."

The bartender figures that maybe he was a little hard on the guy the day before and decides to give the guy the benefit of the doubt. He makes the drinks and they all say, *"Cheers!"* and down the drinks.

The bartender says, "That'll be $42.50."

The drunk replies by putting his thumb to his nose, wiggling his fingers, and making a loud raspberry noise followed by, "I don't have any money and you can kiss my big butt!"

A Guy Goes Into A Bar

This angers the bartender even more than the first time. He jumps over the bar and beats the hell out of the drunk and throws him out into the street onto his face and kicks him a few times for good measure.

The next day the same drunk walks into the same bar, but before he can say anything the bartender says, "Let me guess: you want to buy the whole bar a drink and I should get one for myself, too, right?"

The drunk replies, "No way, you get too violent when you drink!"

A Guy Goes Into A Bar

A guy goes into a bar on the top of a very tall building. He sits down, orders a huge beer, chugs it, walks over to the window, and jumps out.

Five minutes later, the guy walks into the bar again, orders another huge beer, chugs it, walks over to the window, and jumps out again. Five minutes later, he reappears and repeats the whole thing.

About half an hour later, another guy at the bar stops the first guy and says: "Hey, how the heck are you doing that?" The first guy responds: "Oh, it's really simple physics. When you chug the beer, it make you all warm inside and, since warm air rises, if you just hold your breath you become lighter than air and float down to the sidewalk." "*Wow!*" exclaims the second man. "I gotta try that!" So he orders a huge beer, chugs it, goes over to the window, jumps out, and splats on the sidewalk below.

The bartender looks over to the first man and says: "You know, Superman, you act like a real jerk when you're drunk."

A Guy Goes Into A Bar

A guy goes into a bar carrying a little black satchel. He sits down at the bar and orders a Scotch and soda. The bartender gives him his drink. He takes a couple of sips, reaches into the bag, and pulls out a little piano. The bartender's curiosity is somewhat piqued, but he says nothing. The guy takes another couple of sips of his drink, reaches into his bag, and pulls out a little stool. The bartender really wonders what is going on now. The guy finally finishes his drink and he reaches into his bag and pulls out a little man, maybe ten inches high. The little man sits down at the piano and starts whacking out the "Twelfth Street Rag." The bartender comes over to him and says, "What the hell are you doing in this dive? With that act you could make a million bucks. What's going on?" The guy says, "Well, I'll tell you the story. I was walking down the beach one day, I was unemployed with nothing to do. I was just wandering around and this bottle washes up at my feet. I looked at it, it seemed to be empty, so I threw it away. It hit a rock and 'puff' out comes a genie. He looked at me and said, 'Thank you, thank you. You have liberated me after ten thousand years in that bottle. I'm going to give you one wish.' And the son of a bitch thought I wished for a ten-inch pianist."

A Guy Goes Into A Bar

A guy goes into a bar and is so tall that he has to duck as he goes through the entrance. He's at least six foot ten, and when he sits at the bar and orders a drink it appears that he's standing. A woman sitting across recognizes him as a professional basketball player and they begin to have a conversation. After a few drinks they go back to his hotel room. He begins to undress, removing his shirt to reveal a Reebok tattoo. He explains, "When I play basketball, the cameras pick up the tattoo and Reebok pays me for the advertisement." Next he takes off his pants to reveal the word *Puma* tattooed on his leg, and he gives the same explanation. Finally, the underwear comes off and the girl sees the word *AIDS* tattooed on his penis. She jumps back, screaming, "You didn't tell me you had AIDS!" The ballplayer says, "Relax, in a minute it's going to say *ADIDAS*."

A guy goes into a bar where a horse behind the bar is serving drinks. The guy is staring at the horse when the horse says, "Hey, buddy? What are you staring at? Haven't you ever seen a horse serving drinks before?"

The guy says, "No, it's not that . . . it's just that I never thought the parrot would sell the place."

A Guy Goes Into A Bar

A guy goes into a bar and hops on a stool. The bartender says. "What'll you have?" The guy says, "Got any soup?" The bartender snarls, "We don't have soup here, we serve drinks, now get out!" The guy hops off the stool and walks out.

The next day, the same guy walks into the same bar, hops on the same stool, looks the bartender in the eye, and asks, "Got any soup?" The bartender, irritated, says, "I told you yesterday, we don't serve soup here, we serve drinks, now *get out!*" The guy jumps off the stool and walks out.

The next day, the same guy walks into the same bar and sits on a stool, looks at the bartender, and asks, "Got any soup?" The bartender, infuriated, pounds his fist on the bar and yells at the guy, "I told you two times, we don't serve soup here, we serve drinks! If you ask me *one more time* for soup I'm going to nail your pecker to the bar! NOW GET OUT!" With that the guy shrugs, hops off the stool, and walks out.

The next day, the guy comes back, hops on a stool, and asks, "Got any nails?" The bartender, puzzled, says, "No." The guy then looks him square in the eye and says, "Got any soup?"

A Guy Goes Into A Bar

A guy goes into a bar with a little yellow long-nosed, short-legged dog under his arm.

"That's one ugly dog," says another patron while petting his own dog, a Doberman.

"Yeah," says the guy, "but he's a mean little SOB."

"That so," says the other patron. "Bet $20 my dog will kick his ass in less than two minutes."

The guy agrees and they put their dogs face to face, and each gives the command to attack. In the twinkling of an eye the little yellow dog bites the Doberman in half. The Doberman's owner is crying and cussing and screams, "What kind of damn dog is this?"

"Well," says the guy, "before I cut off his tail and painted him yellow he was an alligator."

A Guy Goes Into A Bar

An aardvark goes into a bar. The bartender runs to the boss and says, "There's an aardvark out there, what should I do?" The boss says, "Aardvarks are really stupid. Charge him lots of money for anything he orders." The bartender returns to the counter, where the aardvark orders a beer. The bartender gets it for him and charges him $40. The aardvark is sipping his beer and the bartender, overcome by curiosity, says, "You know, we don't get many aardvarks in here." The aardvark says, "Well, at forty bucks a beer I can see why."

A Guy Goes Into A Bar

A guy goes into a bar, sits down, and starts dialing numbers . . . like a telephone . . . on his open hand, then puts his palm up against his cheek and begins talking. Suspicious, the bartender walks over and tells him this is a very tough neighborhood and he doesn't need any trouble here. The guy says, "You don't understand. I'm very high-tech. I had a phone installed in my hand because I was tired of carrying the cellular." The bartender says, "Prove it." The guy dials up a number and hands his hand to the bartender. The bartender talks into the hand and carries on a conversation. "That's incredible!" says the bartender. "I would never have believed it!" "Yeah," says the guy, "I can keep in touch with my broker, my wife, you name it. By the way, where is the men's room?" The bartender directs him to the men's room. The guy goes in and five, ten, twenty minutes go by and he doesn't return. Fearing the worst given the neighborhood, the bartender goes into the men's room to check on the guy. The guy is spread-eagled up against the wall. His pants are pulled down and he has a roll of toilet paper up his butt. "Oh, my God!" says the bartender. "Did they rob you? Are you hurt?" The guy turns and says, "No, no, I'm okay. I'm just waiting for a fax."

A Guy Goes Into A Bar

A guy goes into a bar wearing a black coat, a black hat, and a scraggly beard peculiar to a certain sect of Hasidic Judaism. He sits next to a Chinese man and both, without saying a word to each other, proceed to get stinking drunk. All of a sudden the Jew turns and punches the Chinese in the face, knocking him off his stool. Stunned, the Chinese gets up and says, "What the hell was that for?" The Jew replies, "That was for Pearl Harbor." The Chinese says, "That was the Japanese, I'm Chinese." The Jew says, "Chinese, Japanese, it's all the same to me."

They both continue to drink, and about a half hour later the Chinese turns and punches the Jew in the face, knocking him off his stool. The Jew gets up and says, "What the hell was that for?" The Chinese says, "That was for the *Titanic*." The Jew replies, "The *Titanic?* That was an iceberg." The Chinese says, "Iceberg, Goldberg, it's all the same to me."

A Guy Goes Into A Bar

A guy goes into a bar one night and asks for a beer. "Certainly, sir. That'll be one cent," says the bartender. "One penny?" exclaims the guy. The bartender nods his head. So the guy glances over at the menu and he asks, "Could I have a nice juicy T-bone steak with french fries and a tossed salad?" "Certainly sir," replies the bartender. "How much money?" inquires the guy. "Four cents," the bartender replies. "Four cents?" exclaims the guy. "Where's the guy who owns this place?" The bartender replies, "Upstairs with my wife." The guy says, "What's he doing with your wife?" The bartender replies, "Same as what I'm doing to his business."

A guy goes into a bar on his way home from work. The bartender pours him a Guinness and asks him if he wants to buy a raffle ticket.

"What's it for?" asks the guy.

"It's for a poor widow with thirteen kids," says the bartender.

The guy shakes his head. "No good to me. I couldn't afford to keep them."

A Guy Goes Into A Bar

A guy goes into a bar and orders three separate shots of Irish whiskey. He downs one, engages in casual conversation with the bartender, eventually finishing the other two. This goes on for a few days, and the bartender finally says, "You know, I can put all three shots in one glass for you." The guy replies, "No, I prefer it this way. See, I'm very close to my two brothers. They're both in Ireland now, and this represents a drink for each of us. This way I can be closer to them and feel like we are all having a drink together."

This goes on for several months and then one day, the guy orders two shots. Well, the bartender begins to worry that maybe something has happened to one of his brothers. "Is everything all right?" the bartender asks. "What do you mean?" replies the guy. "Well," the bartender says, "all these months you've ordered three drinks. Now you've only ordered two. Something didn't happen to one of your brothers, did it?"

"No," the gentleman replies. "They're okay. It's just that I quit drinking."

A Guy Goes Into A Bar

A guy goes into a bar. He is very scrawny, has thick eyeglasses, and is wearing an ugly polyester suit. This bar's so sure that its bartender is the strongest man around that they offer a standing $1,000 bet. The bartender squeezes a lemon until all the juice runs into a glass, then hands the lemon to a patron. Anyone who can squeeze one more drop of juice out wins the money. Many people have tried over time (weight lifters, longshoremen, etc.), but nobody can do it.

The little man in a tiny, squeaky voice says, "I'd like to try the bet."

After the laughter dies down, the bartender says okay, grabs a lemon, and squeezes away. Then he hands the wrinkled remains of the rind to the little man. But the crowd's laughter turns to total silence as the man clenches his fist around the lemon and six drops fall into the glass. As the crowd cheers, the bartender pays the $1,000 and asks the little man, "What do you do for a living? Are you a lumberjack, a weight lifter, or what?"

The man replies, "I work for the IRS."

A Guy Goes Into A Bar

A guy goes into a bar with a Seeing Eye dog. Although blind the man reaches the center of the bar without a problem, snatches the dog up by the tail and starts swinging him around and around. The bartender speaks up and says, "Hey, what the hell are you doing?"

The blind man says, "Just taking a look around."

A Guy Goes Into A Bar

A guy goes into a bar, glances over, and sees a man that looks just like Hitler. He decides that he had better inform the man of this before he goes out and gets beat up.

"Excuse me sir," says the man, "but I just thought that I'd let you know that you look just like Hitler and you better be careful where you walk." The other man looks up and says, "Oh, that's because I *am* Hitler."

The man is stunned and asks, "Did you just say that you are Hitler?" "Yes, that is what I said. You see, I've been hiding out in Bolivia and reassembling my army to take over the world. First we're going to kill all the Jews, then we're going to kill all the baseball players."

Again the man looks puzzled. Then he asks, "Why are you going to kill the baseball players?" The other man exclaims, "See, I always said nobody cared about the Jews!!!!"

A Guy Goes Into A Bar

An old man goes into a bar and proceeds to order tequila after tequila. After a while he yells at the bartender, "Bartender, get me another tequila!" The bartender gets him the tequila. The old man drinks it as fast as he can. Then he looks around the bar and sees three large men at a table having some beers. He points at one of them and says, "You! I slept with your mother!" The man looks at the old man, then goes about drinking his beer. Then the old man yells, "Bartender! Get me another tequila!" The bartender gets him another tequila. The old man drinks it as fast as he can. Then he looks over at the three men. He points at another man and shouts, "You! I had oral sex with your mother!" The second man looks at the old man, then goes about drinking his beer. Then the old man yells, "Bartender! Get me another tequila!" This time the bartender says, "No, old man, you have had enough." "Just one more!" yells the old man. So the bartender gets him one more tequila. The old man drinks it as fast as he can. Then he looks at the three men. He points at the third man and shouts, "You! I've been sleeping with your mother for years!" The third man looks at the old man, then looks at the other two men.

All three of them get up and start walking over to the old man. Then they say, "Come on, Dad, you've had too much to drink!"

A Guy Goes Into A Bar

A termite walks into a bar and says, "Is the bar tender here?"

A guy goes into a bar and observes an Englishman, a Scotsman, and an Irishman each being served a pint of Guinness. Just as they are about to enjoy their creamy beverage, a fly lands in each of their pints and becomes stuck in the thick head. The Englishman pushes his beer from him in disgust.

The Irishman fishes the offending fly out of his beer and continues drinking it as if nothing had happened.

The Scotsman picks the fly out of his drink, holds it out over the beer, and yells, *"Spit it out!! Spit it out you bastard!!!!!"*

A Guy Goes Into A Bar

A guy goes into a bar that is located directly across the street from a hospital. The guy, a doctor, has a regular habit of stopping off at the bar for a hazelnut daiquiri on his way home. The bartender knows of his habit and always has the drink waiting at precisely 5:30 P.M. One afternoon, as the end of the workday approaches, the bartender is dismayed to find that he is out of hazelnuts. Thinking quickly, he throws together a daiquiri made with hickory nuts and sets it on the bar. The doctor comes in at his regular time, takes one sip of the drink, and exclaims, "This isn't a hazelnut daiquiri!" "No, I'm sorry," replies the bartender. "It's a hickory daiquiri, doc."

A Guy Goes Into A Bar

A guy goes into a bar with an alligator and asks the bartender, "Do you serve IRS agents here?"

"Of course," he says.

"Good, give me a beer, and give the agent to my 'gator!"

A Guy Goes Into A Bar

A guy goes into a bar with a dog under his arm. He puts the dog on the bar and announces that the dog can talk and that he has $100 he's willing to bet anyone who says he can't. The bartender takes the bet and the owner looks at the dog and asks, "What's the thing on top of this building which keeps the rain from coming inside?" The dog answers, "*Roof.*" The bartender says, "Who are you kidding. I'm not paying." The dog owner says, "How about double or nothing and I'll ask him something else."

The bartender agrees, and the owner turns to the dog and asks, "Who was the greatest ballplayer of all time?" The dog answers, "*Roof.*" With that the bartender picks them both up and throws them out the door.

As they bounce on the sidewalk the dog looks at his owner and says, "DiMaggio?"

A Guy Goes Into A Bar

A guy goes into a bar. He's a rather large construction worker with a menacing glare. He orders a beer, chugs it back, and bellows, "All you guys on the right side of the bar are queers!" A sudden silence descends. After a moment he asks, "Anyone got a problem with that?" No one says a word. He then chugs back another beer and growls, "And all you guys on the left side of the bar are mother@#$%!" Once again the bar is silent. He looks around belligerently and roars, "Anyone got a problem with that?" A lone man on the left side of the bar gets up from his stool unsteadily and starts to walk toward the man. "You got a problem, buddy?" "Oh no, I'm just on the wrong side of the bar."

A Guy Goes Into A Bar

A guy goes into a bar and stumbles up to the only other patron there and asks if he can buy him a drink. "Why, of course," comes the reply.

The first man then asks, "Where are you from?" "I'm from Ireland," replies the second man. The first man responds, "You don't say, I'm from Ireland too! Let's have another round to Ireland." "Of course," replies the second man. Curious, the first man then asks, "Where in Ireland are you from?" "Dublin," comes the reply. "I can't believe it," says the first man, "I'm from Dublin too! Let's have another drink to Dublin." "Of course," replies the second man. Curiosity again strikes and the first man asks, "What school did you go to?" "Saint Mary's," replies the second man. "I graduated in 'sixty-two." "This is unbelievable," the first man says. "I went to Saint Mary's and I graduated in 'sixty-two, also!"

At about that time in comes one of the regulars and sits down at the bar.

"What's been going on?" he asks the bartender.

"Nothing much," replies the bartender. "The O'Malley twins are drunk again."

A Guy Goes Into A Bar

A brain walks into a bar and says, "I'll have a beer." The bartender looks at him and says, "Sorry, I can't serve you." "Why not?" asks the brain. "You're already out of your head."

A Guy Goes Into A Bar

A guy goes into a bar, walks up to the bartender, and says, "I bet you $300 that I can pee standing from here all the way into that glass"—which is ten feet away—"over there without spilling a single drop!" The bartender says, "You're telling me you can pee standing over here, all the way over there into that glass without spilling a single drop?" The guy nods yes. The bartender says, "Okay, you got yourself a deal!"

The guy unzips, looks at the glass, and begins to pee. He's peeing *all* over the place. He's peeing on the phone, he's peeing on the wall, he's peeing on the bar, and even on the bartender. He's peeing everywhere except the glass. But the bartender is laughing his ass off, he's $300 richer! With pee dripping down his face, he goes, "You stupid *idiot!* You peed everywhere except the glass! You owe me $300!"

The guy goes to the back of the bar, where a couple of guys are playing pool. He collects some money from them and comes back with a big smile on his face. He pays the bartender $300. The bartender looks at him and says, "Why are you so happy? You just lost $300?!" The guy goes, "You see those guys back there playing pool? Yesterday I bet them $500 apiece that I could pee on your phone, pee on your wall, pee on your bar, and pee on *you*, and not only would you not be mad about it, you'd be happy!"

A Guy Goes Into A Bar

A guy goes into a bar and sees a sign on top of the mirror that reads WORD BAR. He asks the woman behind the counter, "What's all this Word Bar stuff?" She says, "Exactly what it says: we've got verbs, prepositions, hyperbole, punctuation—whatever you want." "Okay," says the guy, "gimme an entendre." "Single or double?" she asks. "Make it a double!" She raises one eyebrow and looks him up and down with a sly grin and says, "Don't you mean a *large* one?"

A guy goes into a bar and sits next to a gorgeous woman. He buys her a drink and then another and then another. After this and the accompanying small talk, he asks her back to his place for a "good time." "Look," says the woman, "what do you think I am? I don't turn into a slut after three drinks, you know!" "Okay, okay," replies the guy. "So how many does it take?"

A Guy Goes Into A Bar

A guy goes into a bar, sits down, and claims he knows everyone in the world. The guy sitting next to him says, "I don't believe you—do you know me?" The first guy says, "Sure, Phil, we met two years ago at a convention. My name is Tony, remember?" The second guy says, "Okay, I remember, but I still don't believe you know everyone." So he asks Tony if he knows the bartender. Tony and the bartender, of course, go way back. The bartender confirms this. Phil tries to think of someone Tony couldn't possibly know. So he says to Tony, "Do you know Bill Clinton?" Tony replies, "Oh, yeah. Bill and I smoked dope back at Oxford together." To prove it, he calls Bill Clinton on the president's private line. The two have a twenty-minute conversation. Phil is now determined to come up with someone Tony would never be able to know.

This time he says, "How about the pope?" The only way to prove this is to go to the Vatican. Tony and Phil get on a plane and fly to the Vatican. At the Vatican Tony requests an audience with the pope, and, much to Phil's surprise, is immediately granted one. Tony goes inside and in a few minutes appears on the balcony with the pope. They seem like old friends. Phil can hardly believe his own eyes. He's almost ready to concede that Tony knows everyone when a little guy in the crowd taps him on the shoulder and asks, "Excuse me, but who is that guy on the balcony standing next to Tony?"

A Guy Goes Into A Bar

A guy goes into a bar and sits down. After a few minutes, he sees a beautiful woman sitting at the other end of the bar reading a book, so he tells the bartender to send her a beer. The bartender sets the beer down in front of her, but she doesn't pay any attention to it and continues reading. The guy is a little disturbed, so he tells the bartender to send another beer, but again, she ignores it and continues reading. The guy thinks to himself, "Maybe I should try one more time." So he tells the bartender to send her one more beer, but again she ignores it and keeps reading.

Now the guy is getting a little upset, so he decides to go talk to this woman. He walks up and says, "Excuse me, miss, but I just bought you three beers and you ignored all of them. May I ask why?" She replies, "I'm sorry, I was too wrapped up in this book about male genitalia. Did you know that American Indian men have the widest, fattest penises?" "Um, no, I didn't know that." "And did you know that Mexicans have the longest penises of any men." "Nope, didn't know that." The woman then extends her hand and says, "My name is Cathy, what's yours?" "Tonto Rodriguez!"

A Guy Goes Into A Bar

A guy goes into a bar and has a few drinks too many. Later he has to go to the bathroom and asks where the bathroom is. The bartender says, "Down the hall, take your first right." So the guy goes into the bathroom and sees this golden toilet. He takes care of business and leaves. The next day the same guy goes back to the bar and has a couple of drinks again. A little while later the guy says, "Hey, do you still have that golden toilet?" The bartender turns around and yells, "Hey, Murphy, I found the guy who crapped in your tuba!"

Two cartons of yogurt walk into a bar. The bartender says to them, "We don't serve your kind in here." One of the yogurt cartons says back to him, "Why not? We're cultured individuals."

A Guy Goes Into A Bar

A guy goes into a bar, looks around, and then tells the bartender he wants to buy a round for the house. As the bartender starts to fix the drinks, he asks the guy, "What's the occasion?" The guy says he just finished a jigsaw puzzle in record time. The bartender asks, "How long did it take you?" The guy says, "Just under nineteen hours!!!" The bartender says, "How many pieces were there?" The guy says, "Fifteen!!" The bartender says, "I sure wouldn't go around bragging about that!!" "*Why not?*" he says. "The box said it was for five to seven years!"

A Guy Goes Into A Bar

A shrimp goes into a bar, and after a little while a crab comes up to buy her a drink. They start talking and soon fall madly in love. They begin to date regularly, and everything's going great untill the shrimp tells her father that she's dating a handsome young crab and wants to introduce him to the family. "I'll never allow a crab in this house!" the father responds angrily. "Crabs can't even walk straight, and I forbid you to ever see him again."

Devastated, the shrimp sends off a tear-stained letter informing the crab that she has to break off the relationship, then cries herself to sleep. But later that night she hears a terrible banging on the door and goes downstairs to investigate. It's the crab standing at the door with a wild look in his eyes. "You can't stay here," she says. "My father won't allow it."

"Stand aside," he bellows and walks right into the house. But much to her amazement he's no longer walking crooked. "Why, why . . . you're walking straight," she says.

"Shut up," he answers, "I'm drunk!"

A Guy Goes Into A Bar

A guy goes into a bar and sits on a stool next to a smaller fellow. The smaller guy looks at the first guy, grabs him by the arms and neck, and says, "That's a choke hold from judo." The first guy, figuring that the little guy is just a bit drunk, lets it slide. Two minutes later, he finds himself in another hold, and the little fellow says, "That's a secret bracing hold in karate." Now the guy is getting a little steamed, but he lets it pass. Five minutes later, the little fellow jumps on him again and puts him in another compromising position. He says, "That's a death move in tae kwon do." Now the guy is angry and quickly leaves the bar. Ten minutes later he comes back into the bar, and the little fellow is still at the bar waiting for another drink. The guy walks up to him, and before the little fellow can move, he lunges at him, his arm flying out from behind his back. The little fellow falls off of his stool and is out cold. The first guy turns to the bartender and says, "That was a monkey wrench from Sears!"

A Guy Goes Into A Bar

A guy goes into a bar and is having a few drinks when he notices a very attractive lady siting down at the other end of the bar ordering a drink. The guy calls the bartender over and says "Whatever she's drinking, give her another one and tell her it's on me." The bartender replies, "I don't think you want to do that." "What do you mean?" yells the guy. "Send her the drink!" "Okay," the bartender replies, "but I don't think it is a good idea." "And why not?" asks the guy indignantly. The bartender leans over the bar and very softly says, "Because she's a lesbian." "I don't care, send her a drink."

After the lady gets her drink the guy very casually strolls down to the other end of the bar and sits down next to her and says, "*So,* what part of Lesbia are *you* from?"

A Guy Goes Into A Bar

A guy goes into a bar, obviously already intoxicated, and sets himself down. After being served he notices a woman sitting a few stools down. He motions the bartender over and says, "Bartender, I'd like to buy that old douche bag down there a drink." Somewhat offended, the bartender replies, "Sir, I run a respectable establishment, and I don't appreciate your calling my female customers douche bags." The man looks ashamed of himself and mutters, "You're right, that was uncalled for . . . please allow me to buy the woman a cocktail." "That's better," says the bartender and he approaches the woman. "Ma'am, the gentleman down the bar would like to buy you a drink. What would you like?" "How nice!" replies the woman. "I'll have a vinegar and water."

A Guy Goes Into A Bar

A guy goes into a bar, which in itself is an accomplishment as he is totally armless. He orders a drink and, when served, asks the bartender if he would get the money from his wallet in his pocket, since he has no arms. He then asks if the bartender would tip the glass to his lips. He then asks if the bartender would get a hanky from his pocket and wipe the foam from his lips. The bartender does it and comments that it must be very difficult not to have arms and have to ask someone to do nearly everything for him. The man says, "Yes, it is a bit embarrassing at times. By the way, where is your rest room?" The bartender quickly replies, "The closest one is in the gas station three blocks down the street."

A Guy Goes Into A Bar

A guy goes into a bar. He sees an attractive person of the opposite gender and walks up to her. He says, "Hey, can I buy you a drink?" The gal stands up, walks to the middle of the room, and shouts, *"What do you think I am, a prostitute?"* She storms out of the bar and the guy, face completely red, orders a beer and sits in a dark corner, embarrassed by her words. A few minutes later the girl returns and comes up to the guy. She says, "I'm sorry about that. I'm a psychology major and I was just testing to see your reaction to what I said." The guy stands up and walks to the middle of the bar and shouts, *"Fifty dollars! Are you crazy?"*

A Guy Goes Into A Bar

A guy goes into a bar after work to meet his drinking buddy for a couple of beers. They are both airplane mechanics and proceed to talk shop while they drink. The bartender, after giving many warnings, kicks the two mechanics out of the bar for talking loud and acting rowdy. With no place to go, they end up in a hangar at Los Angeles International Airport. One of them says to the other, "Man, have you got anything to drink?" "No, but I hear you can drink jet fuel—that'll kinda give you a buzz." So they get smashed and have a beautiful time, like only drinking buddies can do. The following morning one of them wakes up, and he expects his head to explode when he gets up. But it doesn't. He gets up and feels good; in fact, he feels great—no hangover! The phone rings. It's his buddy, who asks, "Hey, how do you feel?" He says, "I feel great!" The buddy says, "I feel great too!! You don't have a hangover?" He answers, "No—that jet fuel is great stuff—no hangover. We ought to do this more often." "Yeah, we should, but there's just one thing . . . did you fart yet?" "No . . . ???" "Well, don't, 'cause I'm in Boston!!"

A Guy Goes Into A Bar

A sea anenome goes into a bar and says to the bartender, "I'd like to buy a drink for the man in the corner."

The bartender takes the drink to the man in the corner and says, "This is from your friend over there."

The man replies, "With anenome like that, who needs friends?"

A guy goes into a bar, approaches the bartender, and says, "I've been working on a top secret project on molecular genetics for the past five years and I've just got to talk to someone about it."

The bartender says, "Wait a minute. Before we talk about that, just answer a few questions. When a deer defecates, why does it come out like little pellets?"

The guy doesn't know. The bartender then asks, "Why is it that when a dog poops, it lands on the ground and looks like a coiled rope?"

The guy, again, says, "I don't have any idea." The bartender then says, "You don't know crap and you want to talk about molecular genetics?"

A Guy Goes Into A Bar

A guy goes into a bar, slams a twenty down, and tells the bartender he really needs a drink. The bartender serves the drink and asks what's the problem. "I just found out one of my brothers is gay," replies the guy. "Man, that's tough," says the bartender. Two weeks later the same guy comes into the bar again and slams another twenty down. The bartender again inquires about the problem. "I just found out my other brother is gay too!" says the guy. "Wow, your family is screwed up," says the bartender. Two weeks later the guy walks into the bar again. Before he has a chance to take out any money, the bartender looks at him and says, "Hey, doesn't anyone in your family like to sleep with women?" "Yeah," answers the guy, "my wife."

A Guy Goes Into A Bar

A guy goes into a bar, orders a drink, and stares at it for a half hour without moving. A big truck driver finally walks up to him, takes the guy's drink and guzzles it down in one swig. The poor man starts crying. The truck driver says, "Come on, man, I was just joking. Here, I'll buy you another drink. I can't stand seeing a man cry." "No, it's not that. This day is the worst of my life. First, I fall asleep and get to the office late. My boss is outraged, and he fires me. When I leave the building to go to my car, I find out it was stolen. I get a cab to return home, and when I get out I remember I left my wallet and credit cards in my car. I enter my house and I find my wife in bed with the gardener. I leave home and come to this bar. And while I'm thinking about putting an end to my life, you show up and drink my poison . . ."

A Guy Goes Into A Bar

A guy goes into a bar and shouts, "When I drink, everybody drinks!"

He gets a cheer from everybody in the bar.

Feeling pretty happy, he shouts out, "When I drink again, everybody drinks again!"

Again, he gets a cheer, but this one louder.

Upon finishing his drink, he pulls out his wallet and shouts, "When I pay, everybody pays!"

A guy goes into a bar and says, "Bartender, give me a drink, I'm celebrating my fifth wedding anniversary." The bartender comes over and says, "Sure, kid, the drink is free. What are you going to do to celebrate?" He says, "Well, I'm going to take my wife to Europe." The bartender says, "You're going to take your wife to Europe for your fifth anniversary, that's pretty good. What are you going to do for your tenth?" The guy says, "I'm going to go and get her."

A Guy Goes Into A Bar

A guy goes into a bar down in Arkansas and orders a grape soda. Surprised, the bartender looks around and says, "You ain't from around here . . . where you from, boy?" The guy says, "I'm from Pennsylvania." The bartender asks, "What do you do up in Pennsylvania?" The guy responds, "I'm a taxidermist." The bartender says, "A taxidermist . . . what the hell is a taxidermist?" The guy says, "I mount dead animals." The bartender smiles and shouts to the whole bar, "It's okay, boys, he's one of us."

A guy goes into a bar, orders a drink, takes a swig, and loudly proclaims, "All lawyers are assholes." At that moment a drunk at the end of the bar says, "Wait a minute, sir, I take umbrage at that remark." The drinker replies, "Why, are you a lawyer?" The inebriate says, "No, I'm an asshole."

A Guy Goes Into A Bar

A guy goes into a bar where he sees a big sign on the door saying: NERDS NOT ALLOWED—ENTER AT YOUR OWN RISK! The bartender comes over to him, sniffs, says he smells kind of nerdy, and asks him what he does for a living. The guy says he drives a truck, and the smell is just from the computers he is hauling. The bartender says okay, truck drivers are not nerds, and serves him a beer.

As he is sipping his beer, a skinny guy walks in with tape around his glasses, a pocket protector with twelve kinds of pens and pencils, and a belt at least a foot too long. The bartender, without saying a word, pulls out a shotgun and blows the guy away. The truck driver asks him why he did that. The bartender says not to worry: the nerds are overpopulating the Silicon Valley and are in season now. You don't even need a license, he says.

So the truck driver finishes his beer, gets back in his truck, and heads back onto the freeway. Suddenly he veers to avoid an accident, and the load shifts. The back door breaks open, and computers spill out all over the freeway. He jumps out and sees a crowd already forming, grabbing up the computers. They are all engineers, accountants, and programmers, wearing the nerdiest clothes he has ever seen. He can't let them steal his whole load so, remembering what happened in the bar, he pulls out his gun and starts blasting away, felling several of them instantly. A highway patrol officer comes zooming up and jumps out of the car screaming at him to stop.

The truck driver says, "What's wrong? I thought nerds were in season."

"Well, sure," says the policeman, "but you can't bait 'em."

A Guy Goes Into A Bar

A guy goes into a bar and says with a stutter, "S-s-say! B-b-bartender, g-g-gimme a b-b-beer." The bartender, who is badly humpbacked, serves him a beer and says, "That will be $2.50, please!" The guy thinks that's pretty high priced and says, "D-d-d-damn! T-t-that's h-h-high!" The bartender says, "Yes, but that's our price, that's what we get!" The guy pays him and drinks it down. He then says, "S-s-say! B-b-bartender, g-g-gimme a w-whiskey, p-p-please!" The bartender serves him a shot of whiskey and says, "That will be $5.00, please!" The guy says, "D-d-d-damn! T-t-that's h-h-high!" The bartender says, "Yes, but that's our price, that's what we get!" The guy pays him, drinks his whiskey, and before leaving he says, "B-b-bartender, th-thanks for n-not m-m-making f-f-fun of my s-s-stuttering w-w-while I w-was in h-h-here!" The bartender replies, "Oh, that's okay! I want to thank you for not making fun of my humpback while you were in here." The guy says, "Oh t-t-that's okay, everything else in t-t-this p-p-place w-was so h-h-high, I th-thought it w-was y-your *ass!*"

A Guy Goes Into A Bar

A guy goes into a bar and notices two lovely young blond women sitting down. He approaches the bartender and says, "Excuse me, I'd like to buy those two ladies a couple of drinks." But the bartender gives him a funny look and answers, "I'm not so sure that is a good idea. You see, they're lesbians." "Sorry, Mr. Bartender, but I don't know what you're talking about." And the bartender responds, "Why don't you go over there and ask them?" So the man walks over to the women and asks, "I hear you are lesbians. What does that mean?" One answers politely, "Well, we like to kiss and play with each other's breasts."

The man yells to the bartender, "Hey, three drinks here for us lesbians!"

A mushroom goes into a bar and sits down at the counter. He's about to order a drink when the bartender takes one look at him and says: "Hey! Get out of here!! We don't serve *mushrooms* in this place!" Stunned, the mushroom exclaims, "Awh, c'mon, I'm a fun-gi!"

A Guy Goes Into A Bar

A guy goes into a bar with a monkey. He orders a Diet Dr. Pepper for himself and a Guinness for the monkey. After they've had a few drinks he asks to play the piano. He's a good piano player and plays requests for the others in the bar.

While he's playing, the monkey is hopping around and dancing on the tables. This amuses everyone except a grumpy guy sitting at the end of the bar. The monkey jumps up on the bar, walks over to the guy, and spits in his beer.

The guy gets up and walks over to the piano and says to the guy, "Do you know your monkey spat in my beer?"

The piano player shakes his head and replies, "Not offhand, could you hum a few bars?"

A Guy Goes Into A Bar

A guy goes into a bar with his pet octopus, sets him up on the bar and says, "I bet anyone in here fifty bucks that my octopus can play any musical instrument you hand him." One guy walks up with a guitar and says, "You're on." He lays his fifty bucks on the bar, and hands over the guitar. The octopus proceeds to tune the strings and begins to play a wonderful rendition of Beethoven's "Moonlight Sonata." Everyone's aghast! The guy collects his fifty bucks.

The next guy brings up a trumpet and lays his money on the bar. The octopus takes it, plays with the valves for a moment, then proceeds to imitate Louis Armstrong playing "Hello, Dolly." The guy collects his money again.

The bartender leaves and comes back a few minutes later with a set of bagpipes and lays his fifty bucks on the bar. The octopus picks it up, turns it around, looks at it some more, turns it over again to get a different perspective. After a few minutes of this the bartender is getting impatient and asks, "What is he waiting for? Why doesn't he start playing?"

The guy looks over and says, "Play it? Hell, he's trying to figure out how to get her pajamas off!"

A Guy Goes Into A Bar

Two Texans go into a bar and sit down at one end. A gorgeous young lady sits down at the other end and orders a martini. Stunned by her beauty, the two guys stare at her for a while, debating whether to approach her. All of a sudden she starts to cough, clutching her throat and beginning to turn blue. One says to the other, "That there gal is having a bad time!" The other agrees and says, "Think we should go help?" "You bet," says the first. And with that they run over and say, "Can you speak?" She shakes her head no. The first guy then asks, "Can you breathe?" She again shakes her head no. With that he pulls up her skirt, pulls down her panties, turns her over, and licks her on the butt. She is so shocked by the act that she coughs up the obstruction and begins to breathe with embarrassed relief. At which point the first Texan looks at his friend and exclaims, "I guess that hind lick maneuver really does work!"

A Guy Goes Into A Bar

A guy goes into a bar after spending two months as a cowboy herding cattle through Texas. He orders up bottle after bottle of rotgut liquor and proceeds to get really wasted. . . . In the process he manages to anger just about everyone in the bar by being offensive and rude.

Finally he finishes up his fifth bottle and decides he's had just about enough. He proceeds to get up and swaggers out of the bar.

He goes outside to untie his horse from the post and he notices someone has painted his horse's testicles a real bright shade of yellow.

This angers him immensely, so he proceeds to bluster back into the bar, slamming the doors open and yelling out at the top of his lungs, "JUST WHO IN SAM HILL PAINTED MY HORSE'S TESTICLES YELLOW!!!"

After everyone in the bar rustles around a bit, a guy in the back of the bar stands up. This guy is *huge,* at least six foot ten, pure muscle. He says to the cowboy, "I did, so what do you got to say about it, boy!!!"

The cowboy looks back at this guy and says, "Oh, I was just going to let you know that the first coat of paint is dry."

A Guy Goes Into A Bar

A guy goes into a bar. He orders a drink, and after a while he needs to visit the john. He does not want anyone to steal his drink, so he puts a sign on it saying, I SPIT IN THIS BEER, DO NOT DRINK!

After a few minutes he returns. There is another sign next to his beer saying, SO DID I.

A string goes into a bar and orders a drink. "Sorry, we don't serve strings," says the bartender. "What? That sucks!" says the string. So the string walks into the bathroom and ties himself in a knot and messes up his ends. He comes back out and approaches the bar again and again orders a drink. "Hey, aren't you that string?" asks the bartender. "No, I'm a frayed knot."

A Guy Goes Into A Bar

A guy goes into a bar smelling like a distillery and flops onto a bar stool next to a priest. The man's tie is stained, his face is plastered with red lipstick, and a half-empty bottle of gin is sticking out of his coat pocket. He opens his newspaper and begins reading. After a few minutes the guy turns to the priest and asks, "Say, Father, what causes arthritis?" "Mister, it's caused by loose living, being with cheap women, too much alcohol, and a feeling of contempt for your fellow man." "Well, I'll be damned," the drunk mutters, returning to his paper. The priest, thinking about what he has said, nudges the man and apologizes. "I'm very sorry, I didn't mean to come on so strong. How long have you had arthritis?" "I don't have it, Father. I was just reading here that the pope does."

A Guy Goes Into A Bar

A guy goes into a bar that has a dress code, and the maître d' demands he wear a tie. Discouraged, the guy goes to his car to leave when inspiration strikes: he's got jumper cables in the trunk! So he wraps them around his neck, sort of like a string tie, and returns to the bar. The maître d' is reluctant, but he says to the guy, "Okay, you're a pretty resourceful fellow, you can come in . . . but don't start anything!"

A guy goes into a bar with the left side of his face bruised and bleeding. The bartender asks, "What in the world happened to you?" The guy says, "Oh, I got in a fight with my girlfriend and I called her a two-bit whore." "Yeah?" asks the bartender. "What did she do?" "She hit me with her bag of quarters!"

A Guy Goes Into A Bar

A guy goes into a bar and sees everyone crowded about a table watching a little show. On the table is an upside-down pot and a duck tap-dancing on it. The guy, who happens to own a circus, is so impressed that he offers to buy the duck from its owner. After some wheelin' and dealin' they settle on $10,000 for the duck and the pot.

Three days later the circus owner runs back to the bar in anger. "Your duck is a rip-off! I put him on the pot before a whole audience and he didn't dance a single step!"

"So?" asks the duck's former owner. "Did you remember to light the candle under the pot?"

A Guy Goes Into A Bar

A pony goes into a bar and says, "Bartender, may I have a drink?" The bartender says, "What? I can't hear you, speak up!"

"May I please have a drink?"

"What? You have to speak up!"

"Could I please have a drink?"

"Now listen, if you don't speak up I will not serve you."

"I'm sorry, I'm just a little hoarse."

A guy goes into a bar and, after having a few drinks, notices a tiny little spot on the wall that seems to be moving. He calls it to the bartender's attention. The bartender glances at it and says, "It's a ladybug." After a moment of stunned silence the customer says, "Good Lord, what incredible eyesight you have!"

A Guy Goes Into A Bar

A guy goes into a bar, orders a martini, and strikes up a conversation with an attractive woman sitting next to him. "This is a special day," he says, "I'm celebrating." "I'm celebrating, too," she replies, clinking glasses with him. "What are you celebrating?" he asks. "For years I've been trying to have a child," she answers. "Today my gynecologist told me I'm pregnant!"

"Congratulations," the man says, lifting his glass. "As it happens, I'm a chicken farmer and for years all my hens were infertile. But today, they're finally fertile."

"How did it happen?"

"I switched cocks."

"What a coincidence," she says, smiling.

This guy goes into a bar with a frog on his head. The bartender says, "Hey, what's that?" To which the frog replies, "I don't know. It started as a wart on my ass and this is what happened."

A Guy Goes Into A Bar

A guy goes into a bar and orders a martini. When he finishes it, he starts nibbling on the rim of the glass. He keeps nibbling and nibbling until there is nothing left but the stem of the glass. He then throws the stem over his shoulder, where it breaks into pieces on the floor. By now quite a few of the patrons are watching.

He orders another martini and repeats the performance; nibbling the rim of the glass around and around until there is nothing left but the stem, which he throws over his shoulder.

He orders a third martini and does it all over again; nibbling down to the stem and again throwing the stem over his shoulder.

After the fourth time he pays his bill aind leaves. All of the other customers are staring at him in amazement.

The bartender says, "That's the weirdest thing I've ever seen!"

"Yeah," says a customer, "he's throwing away the best part!"

A Guy Goes Into A Bar

A guy goes into a bar and meets a woman and they both begin drinking. Soon they get into an argument about who enjoys sex more. The man says, "Men obviously enjoy sex more than women. Why do you think we're so obsessed with it?" "That doesn't prove anything," the woman counters. "Think about this: when you ear itches and you put your little finger in it and wiggle it around then pull it out, which feels better, your ear or your finger?"

A Guy Goes Into A Bar

A guy goes into a bar after work and stays until the bar closes at 2:00 A.M., at which time he is extremely drunk. When he enters his house he doesn't want to wake anyone, so he takes off his shoes and starts tip-toeing up the stairs. Halfway up the stairs he falls over backward and lands flat on his rear end. That wouldn't be so bad, except that he has a couple of empty pint bottles in his back pockets and they break, and the broken glass carves up his buttocks terribly. But he's so drunk that he doesn't know he's hurt. A few minutes later, as he is undressing, he notices blood, so he checks himself out in the mirror, and, sure enough, his behind is cut up something terrible. Well, he repairs the damage as best he can under the circumstances, and he goes to bed. The next morning, his head is hurting, and his rear is hurting, and he is hunkering under the covers trying to think up some good story when his wife comes into the bedroom.

"Well, you really tied one on last night," she says. "Where'd you go?"

"I worked late," he says, "and I stopped off for a couple of beers."

"A couple of beers? That's a laugh," she replies. "You got plastered last night. Where the hell did you go?"

A Guy Goes Into A Bar

"What makes you so sure I got drunk last night, anyway?"

"Well," she replies, "my first big clue was when I got up this morning and found a bunch of Band-Aids stuck to the mirror."

A bear walks into a bar and asks for a drink. The bartender says, "I'm sorry, we don't serve bears." The bear demands a drink, but the bartender keeps refusing. Finally the bear, glancing over at a woman sitting on a stool near him says, "Either give me a drink, or I'll bite off the arm of this woman sitting next to me." The bartender still refuses, so the bear leans over and bites off her arm. "Now, get me a drink or I'll bite off her other arm too." The bartender says, "Sorry, man, it's just not our policy to serve bears." So the bear takes off her other arm. "Now get me a drink, or else I'll finish her off." But the bartender says no again, so the bear turns around, eats the rest of the woman, and says, "Now get me a drink, or you're next." The bartender shrugs, "Sorry, we don't serve people who take drugs." The bear says, "I haven't taken any drugs." But the bartender replies, "Well, that was a barbiturate."

A Guy Goes Into A Bar

A guy goes into a bar to meet his old army buddy, and after spending a happy evening drinking together, the two G.I.s promise to meet again in ten years at the same bar, same time.

Ten years later the first guy walks in, looks around, and sure enough, there is his old buddy on a bar stool. He clasps his hand and cries, "The day we left I didn't think I'd really see you here!"

The buddy looks up, stares, sways slightly, and asks, "Who left?"

A Guy Goes Into A Bar

A guy goes into a bar to buy some cigarettes for his wife. At the farthest end of the bar he sees a beautiful woman and starts talking to her. They have a couple of beers and one thing leads to another and they end up in her apartment. After they've had their fun, he realizes it's 3:00 A.M. and says, "Oh, no, it's so late, my wife's going to kill me. Have you got any talcum powder?" She gives him some talcum powder, which he proceeds to rub on his hands, and then he goes home. His wife is waiting for him in the doorway, and she is pretty angry. "Where the hell have you been?!!" "Well, honey, it's like this. I went to the store like you asked, but they were closed. So I went to the bar to use the vending machine. I saw this great-looking chick there and we had a few drinks and one thing led to another and I ended up in bed with her." "Oh, yeah? Let me see your hands!" She sees his hands are covered with powder and . . . "You God damn liar!!! You went bowling again!!!"

A Guy Goes Into A Bar

A guy goes into a bar and sits down to have a drink. He notices that at the other end of the bar is the most attractive woman he has ever seen. He is immediately lust-struck and decides that he must have her. He leans over to the bartender and asks if the bartender has any Spanish Fly in the back. The bartender says he will check and comes back a couple of minutes later with a small packet of white powder. He says to the man, "We are all out of Spanish Fly, but this is Jewish Fly, and it is guaranteed to get her over here within twenty minutes after she takes it!" The man forks over $10 and asks the bartender to mix the Jewish Fly into a champagne cocktail and deliver it to the woman with his compliments.

The woman drinks the champagne cocktail and looks at our hero rather disinterestedly, but about twenty minutes later she slinks off her bar stool. She saunters across the room in a most seductive manner, oozing sensuality. She reaches him and puts one lithe arm around his shoulders and leans in close to his ear. He can feel her breath on his neck as she whispers, "Hey, big boy . . . want to go shopping?"

A Guy Goes Into A Bar

A guy goes into a bar with a dachshund under his arm. The dog is wearing a New Orleans Saints jersey and helmet and is festooned with Saints pom-poms. The bartender says, "Hey! No pets are allowed in here! You'll have to leave!" The guy begs him, "Look, I'm desperate. We're both big fans, the TV is broken, and this is the only place around where we can see the game!"

After securing a promise that the dog will behave, and warning him that he and the dog will be thrown out if there's any trouble, the bartender relents and allows them to stay in the bar and watch the game.

The game begins with the Saints receiving the kickoff. They march downfield, get stopped at about the 30, and kick a field goal. With that the dog jumps up on the bar and begins walking up and down the bar, giving high fives to everyone.

The bartender says, "Wow, that is the most amazing thing I've ever seen! What does the dog do if they score a touchdown?"

The owner replies, "I don't know, I've only had him for four years."

A Guy Goes Into A Bar

A guy goes into a bar and sees a bird sitting on a perch. "Hey, bartender," he says, "what kind of bird is that?" "Oh," says the bartender, "that's a Crunch Bird!" "I've never heard of a Crunch Bird," says the guy. "Just watch." The bartender takes a newspaper off the bar and throws it down on the floor, then he turns to the bird and says, "Crunch Bird, my paper!" The bird swoops down and attacks the newspaper. He rips it to shreds until there's nothing left but tiny pieces of confetti. "Wow," says the customer, "can I try?" "Be my guest," the bartender replies.

The customer takes off his shoe and puts it on the bar and says, "Crunch Bird, my shoe!" The bird flies down off the perch and picks the shoe up with his beak. He slams the shoe down on the bar and starts attacking it. In no time, the shoe is reduced to nothing but a few pieces of leather and a shoelace. Then the bird flies back to his perch behind the bar.

Suddenly a tough-looking guy walks into the bar. He yells, "Gimme a drink, *now!*" He looks around the bar, snarling, and yells at the patrons, "What the hell are you clowns looking at?" The bar is completely silent. Then the bully notices the bird and says, "What the hell kind of stupid-looking bird is that?" "That's a Crunch Bird," says the bartender.

The tough guy laughs and yells, "Crunch Bird, my ass!"

A Guy Goes Into A Bar

A seal goes into a bar and asks the bartender for a drink. The bartender asks the seal, "What's your pleasure?" The seal replies, "Anything but Canadian Club."

A guy goes into a bar, where he meets a nice, single girl. They have a few drinks and soon wind up at his place in bed. They're having a great time. She is on top when suddenly she has a seizure—she's shaking uncontrollably. Our uninformed male thinks this is incredible—the best sex he's ever had. He finishes, but she's still shaking and thrashing about with her seizure. He begins to get nervous and takes her to the emergency room. A nurse asks what the girl's problem is, and he replies, "Er . . . I think her orgasm is stuck!"

A Guy Goes Into A Bar

A guy goes into a bar and sits down next to a drunk who is closely examining something held in his fingers. The guy watches the drunk for a while, until he finally gets curious enough to ask what it is.

"Well," says the drunk, "it looks like plastic and feels like rubber."

"Let me have it," says the man. Taking it, he begins to roll it between his thumb and forefinger, examining it closely. "Yes," he finally says, "it does look like plastic and feel like rubber, but I don't know what it is. Where did you get it?"

"From my nose," the drunk replies.

A Guy Goes Into A Bar

A guy goes into a bar dragging a horse behind him. The horse orders a whiskey, the guy orders water. When the horse is finished, he orders another. The man nurses his water. When the horse is on his second bottle, the man is still drinking his water. Finally the bartender says, "Are you sure I can't get you a drink?" "No, thanks," says the man, "I'm driving."

A Guy Goes Into A Bar

A guy goes into a bar and orders drink after drink and soon passes out. Another guy, amused by his immoderation, peels the label off his beer bottle and sticks it on the poor chap's forehead. An hour or so later, the guy awakens, looks at his watch, and thinks, "Oh, man! . . . I better get home *now!*"

He hasn't even gone a mile when he sees red lights flashing in his rearview mirror. "Oh, *damn!*" he says as he pulls over. The officer walks up, looks in, and asks, "Sir . . . have you been drinking?" "Well, I had one or two," comes the slurred reply. Disgusted, the cop says, "Why, sir, do you have a Budweiser label on your *face?*"

The fellow looks at himself in the mirror . . . he has no recollection. His mind racing, he suddenly smiles, looks at the cop, and says, "Oh *this?* Well, you see, I'm trying to quit drinking, and my doctor gave me this *patch!*"

A horse goes into a bar. The bartender looks at him and says, "Why the long face?"

A Guy Goes Into A Bar

A guy goes into a bar followed by his fellow bass players. It seems an orchestra was playing Beethoven's Ninth Symphony and the bass section had a twenty-minute break between parts, so the conductor gave them permission to leave the stage during the part of the performance where they were not needed. So the basses left the stage and went across the street to the bar for a beer. Then it became two beers, and three. Finally, someone says they should head back, but the head bass player says, "Don't worry. Before the concert I used a piece of string to tie the last pages of the score together. The conductor will have to slow down the symphony until he unties the score with his free hand." So after another few beers, the basses return to the concert hall, just in time to see the conductor trying to untie the score. He gives them a stern look when he sees them stumble in. After all, it was the bottom of the Ninth, the score was tied, and the basses were loaded.

A guy goes into a bar carrying an ape in his arms. "I just bought this fella as a pet," he explains. "We have no children, so he's going to live with us just like one of the family. He'll eat at our table, even sleep in the bed with me and the wife."

"But what about the smell?" someone asks.

"Oh, he'll just have to get used to it the same way I did."

A Guy Goes Into A Bar

A guy goes into a bar, has a few drinks, and then looks over and notices a drunk guy passed out at a table nearby. The bartender tells him the drunk is Mr. Murphy and asks the man if he can drive Mr. Murphy home. Being a Good Samaritan, the man agrees.

The bartender writes down the address and gives it to him. The man walks over and tries to wake Mr. Murphy, but Mr. Murphy is groggy and quite drunk. The man helps Mr. Murphy to his feet and Mr. Murphy falls to the floor in a heap. "Jeez," the man says, wondering how anyone could drink so much. He takes Mr. Murphy by the arm and practically drags him out to the car. Once there he leans him against the side of his car while he looks for his keys. Mr. Murphy slides down to the ground. The man finds his keys and manages to get Mr. Murphy positioned in the car.

He then drives to the address the bartender gave him. He opens the passenger door and helps Mr. Murphy out and the guy falls to the ground. Cursing softly now, the man helps him to his feet and practically drags him to the front door. He lets go of Mr. Murphy to knock on the door and the guy falls down again. He helps him to his feet as Mrs. Murphy answers the door. "Hi, Mrs. Murphy. Your husband had a little too much to drink tonight, so I gave him a ride home." "That was nice of you," she says looking around, "but where's his wheelchair?"

A Guy Goes Into A Bar

A guy goes into a bar and spies a beautiful woman sitting at a table in the corner. "May I buy you a drink?" he asks. "Okay, but it won't do you any good." A little later he asks, "May I buy you another drink?" "Okay, but it won't do you any good." He invites her up to his apartment and she replies, "Okay, but it won't do you any good." They get to his apartment and he says, "You are the most beautiful thing I have ever seen. I want you for my wife." She says, "Oh, that's different. Send her in."

A Guy Goes Into A Bar

A snail crawls up to a bar as it is being closed. The snail pounds and pounds on the door until the bartender finally opens up. The bartender looks around and sees nothing, until the snail demands a beer. The bartender looks down and sees him but replies, "Hey, we're closed now, and besides we don't serve snails!" and then proceeds to slam the door. The snail again pounds on the door, until the bartender gets so frustrated that he opens the door again and kicks the snail away.

A year later as the bartender is about to close, he hears a pounding on the door. He opens the door and looks down to see the same snail again. The snail looks up and says, "What'd you do that for?"

A Guy Goes Into A Bar

A guy goes into a bar, sits down cross-legged, and places a turban on his head. At about the same time, a husband and his very attractive wife are out enjoying a round of golf, about to tee off on the third hole. The wife hits her shot and the ball begins to slice. The shot is headed directly at the plate-glass window of the bar. Much to their chagrin, the ball smashes through the window, shattering it into a million pieces. Compelled to see what damage has been done, they drive up to the bar. When they peek inside, all they see is this guy sitting cross-legged on the counter with a turban on his head.

The wife asks, "Pardon me, but do you work here?" "No, someone just hit a ball through that window, knocked over the vase you see there, and freed me from that hideous little bottle. I am so grateful," he answers, bowing his head toward them, The husband asks, "Are you a genie?" "Oh, why yes, I am. In fact, I am so grateful, I will grant you two wishes; the third wish I will keep for myself." The husband's first wish is for a scratch handicap, and the other is for an income of a million dollars a year. "For *my* wish, I would like to have my way with your wife. I have not been with a woman for many years and, after all, I

A Guy Goes Into A Bar

have made you a scratch golfer and millionaire." The husband agrees and his wife goes off with the genie to a nearby room.

After the genie and wife finish, the genie asks the wife if she minds if he asks her a few questions. "No, I don't mind," she replies. "How long have you been married?" She replies, "Three years." The genie then asks, "How old is your husband?" To which she responds, "Forty-one years old." Then the genie asks, "So, how long has he believed in this genie stuff?"

A guy goes into a bar and orders a shot of whiskey. He gulps it down and peeks into his shirt pocket. He orders another shot of whiskey, gulps it down, and peeks into his shirt pocket. He orders a third shot and does the same thing. After the sixth shot, he asks the bartender for the bill, pays, and starts to walk out. Curiosity gets the better of the bartender and he says to the guy, "Excuse me, but I noticed that every time you drank a shot you kept looking into your pocket. I was wondering what's in your pocket."

The guy slurs, "Well, I have a picture of my wife in my pocket. I keep drinking until she starts to look good, then I go home."

A Guy Goes Into A Bar

A guy goes into a bar; he's short and slight, and as he walks up to the counter he slips on some dog's mess on the floor. He picks himself up, orders a drink, and sits down at a table. Shortly afterward a huge guy walks in and slips on the same mess. As he picks himself up, the little guy walks over and says, "I just did that," so the big guy picks him up and rubs his nose in it.

A Guy Goes Into A Bar

A guy goes into a bar with a German shepherd dog and sits down at the counter. The bartender says, "You can't bring that dog in here!" The guy says, "This is a Seeing Eye dog!" The bartender says, "Well, okay, then I guess it can stay."

After a while, the man and the German shepherd get up to leave. As they're going out the door, another man with a Chihuahua is coming in, and the first man says, "The bartender won't like you bringing that dog in here, but just tell him it's a Seeing Eye dog and then it'll be okay." The second man looks dubiously at his tiny Chihuahua, thinks a few seconds, thanks the first man, and goes in.

The bartender says, "Hey! You can't bring that Chihuahua in here!" The man stares straight ahead and exclaims, "What! They sold me a Chihuahua?!"

A Guy Goes Into A Bar

A guy goes into a bar, quickly orders four expensive thirty-year-old single malts and has the bartender line them up in front of him. Then, without pausing, he downs each one.

"Whew," the bartender remarks, "you seem to be in a hurry."

"You would be too if you had what I have."

"What do you have?" the bartender asks sympathetically.

"Fifty cents."

A Guy Goes Into A Bar

A guy goes into a bar. He's a black man and is there to meet his two friends, one of whom is Italian and the other Polish. They sit, order a drink, and are starting to make a little small talk when the black guy sees a man sitting at the end of the bar and says, "Hey, isn't that Jesus sitting at the end of the bar?" The Polish guy says, "It sure looks like him." The Italian says, "Yeah, I think you guys are right. But he looks a little depressed, let's buy him a drink."

So they hail the bartender and tell him to get Jesus a drink. Jesus accepts the drink and finishes it down and then walks over to the guys to thank them.

He walks to the Italian guy first and says, "Thank you, my son" and touches the back of the Italian guy's head. The Italian says, "Hey, my eyesight's better. I can see clearly now! Thank you, Jesus!" The Italian guy proceeds to throw away his glasses.

Jesus then walks up to the Polish guy and touches him on the shoulder and says, "Thank you, my son.

The Polish guy says, "Wow, I can move again. My arthritis is gone! Thank you Jesus!" and the Polish guy jumps for joy. Jesus then goes over to the black guy to thank him. Jesus says, "Thank you, my son."

The black guy jumps back and says, "Wait a minute, don't even think about touching me, Jesus, it's taken me years to get on workmen's comp."

A Guy Goes Into A Bar

A guy goes into a bar, meets his best friend, and they start to talk about their respective married lives. "I had sex with my wife before we were married," says the first guy, "did you?" "Gee, I don't know," answers his friend, "what was your wife's maiden name?"

A Guy Goes Into A Bar

A guy goes into a bar and sits next to a pirate. The landlubber notices that, like any self-respecting pirate, this guy has a peg leg, a hook in place of one of his hands, and a patch over one eye. The landlubber just has to find out how the pirate got in such bad shape. He asks the pirate, "How did you lose your leg?" The pirate responds, "I lost me leg in a battle off the coast of Jamaica!" His new acquaintance is still curious so he inquires, "What about your hand. Did you lose it at the same time?" "No," answers the pirate. "I lost it to the sharks off the Florida Keys." Finally, the landlubber asks, "I notice you also have an eye patch. How did you lose your eye?" The pirate answers, "I was sleeping on a beach when a seagull flew over and crapped right in me eye." The landlubber asks incredulously, "How could a little seagull crap make you lose your eye?" The pirate snaps, "It was the day after I got me hook!"

A Guy Goes Into A Bar

A guy goes into a bar, has a few drinks, and asks what his tab is. "Twenty dollars," the bartender replies. The guy says, "I'll bet you my tab, double or nothing, that I can bite my eye." The bartender accepts and the guy pulls out his glass eye and bites it. He has a few more drinks and asks for his bill again. Thirty dollars plus tip. He bets the bartender he can bite his other eye. The bartender accepts, knowing the guy can't have two glass eyes. The guy takes out his false teeth and bites his other eye.

A ham sandwich goes into a bar. The bartender says, "We don't serve ham sandwiches!" The sandwich says, "That's okay, I just want a drink."

A Guy Goes Into A Bar

This guy goes into a bar with a duck on his head. The bartender, who's seen just about everything, says, "What can I do for you?"

To which the duck replies, "You can start by getting this guy off my ass."

A guy goes into a bar with his buddy, looking for girls.

The first guy says, "Hey, check out the blond over there. I bet she's really hot in bed!" He proceeds to go over and make small talk with her. Before long they both leave for a one-nighter.

The next day, the two guys meet up and are again looking for anything that breathes. The second guy goes over to the same blond, pinches her in the rear, and they go off for a quickie. Fifteen minutes later the second guy comes back and says, "I think my wife is better."

The first guy nods his head and says, "Yeah, your wife *is* better!"

A Guy Goes Into A Bar

A guy goes into a bar followed by his pet giraffe, and they both get totally plastered. The giraffe passes out and the man gets up to leave.

The bartender says, "You can't leave that lyin' there."

The drunk says, "It's not a lion, it's a giraffe."

A Guy Goes Into A Bar

Two guys wander into a bar, One of the men shouts to the bartender, "Hi ya, Mike. Set 'em up for me and my pal here." Then he turns to his slightly dim-witted friend and boasts, "This is a great bar. For every two drinks you buy, the house gives you one. And the pinball machines in the back are free!" "That's not so great," responds the friend. "There's a bar across town that'll match you drink for drink, and you can have sex in the back for free." "Where is this place?" the first guy exclaims. "Oh, I don't know," the dim fellow replies, "but my wife goes there all the time."

A Guy Goes Into A Bar

A guy goes into a bar and sits down next to a man with a dog at his feet. "Does your dog bite?" he asks.

"No," is the reply. A few minutes later the dog takes a huge chunk out of his leg.

"I thought you said your dog doesn't bite!" the guy says indignantly, moaning in great pain.

"I did, but that's not my dog."

A Guy Goes Into A Bar

A panda goes into a bar, sits down and orders a sandwich. He eats the sandwich, pulls out a gun, and shoots the waitress dead. As the panda stands up to go, the bartender shouts, "Hey! Where are you going? You just shot my waitress and you didn't pay for your sandwich!"

The panda yells back at the bartender, "Hey man, I'm a *panda!* Look it up!"

The bartender opens his dictionary and sees the following definition for *panda:* "A tree-dwelling marsupial of Asian origin, characterized by distinct black-and-white coloring. Eats shoots and leaves."

A Guy Goes Into A Bar

A guy goes into a bar smelling and looking like he hasn't had a bath in a month. He orders a drink. The bartender says, "No way, I don't think you can pay for it." The guy says, "You're right. I don't have any money, but if I show you something you haven't seen before, will you give me a drink?" The bartender says, "Sure."

So the guy reaches into his coat pocket and pulls out a hamster. He puts the hamster on the bar and it runs to the end of the bar, down the bar, across the room, up the piano, jumps on the keyboard, and starts playing Gershwin. And the hamster is really good. The bartender says, "You're right. I've never seen anything like that before. That hamster is really good." The guy downs the drink and asks for another. "Money or another something I haven't seen before or else no drink," says the bartender.

The guy reaches into his coat again and pulls out a frog. He puts the frog on the bar, and the frog starts to sing. He has a marvelous voice and great pitch—a fine singer. A stranger from the other end of the bar runs over to the guy and offers him $300 for the frog. The guy says, "It's a deal." He takes the $300 and gives the stranger the frog. The stranger runs out of the bar.

The bartender says to the guy, "Are you some kind of nut? You sold a singing frog for $300? It must have been worth millions. You must be crazy."

"Don't worry," says the guy, "the hamster is a ventriloquist."

A Guy Goes Into A Bar

A guy goes into a bar with a small dog. The bartender says, "Get out of here with that dog!" The guy says, "But this isn't just any dog . . . this dog can play the piano!"

The bartender replies, "Well, if he can play the piano you both can stay . . . and have a drink on the house!"

So the guy sits the dog on the piano stool, and the dog starts playing. Ragtime, Mozart . . . and the bartender and patrons are enjoying the music.

Suddenly, a bigger dog runs in, grabs the small dog by the scruff of the neck, and drags him out. The bartender asks the guy, "What was that all about?"

The guy replies, "Oh, that was his mother. She wants him to be a doctor."

A Guy Goes Into A Bar

A guy goes into a bar, pulls out a syringe, and tells everyone there, "Give me all your money, watches, jewelry, and anything of value or I will inject you with gonorrhea." One by one everyone hands over all their stuff, except for one drunk at the end of the bar.

"I told you to hand over all your stuff or I'll inject you with gonorrhea."

The drunk at the bar says, "Go ahead, I'm wearing a condom."

A Guy Goes Into A Bar

A guy goes into a bar with a big sign that says, FREE BEER FOR LIFE TO THE FIRST PERSON WHO CAN PASS THE THREE CHALLENGES!

"What three challenges?" the guy asks.

"Well ya see," says the bartender, "first, there's a gallon of pepper tequila, and you have to drink the whole thing at once, *and* you can't make a face while doing it. If that doesn't kill you, then there's an alligator out back with a sore tooth, and you need to go out there and remove it with your bare hands. Finally, there's a woman upstairs who's never had an orgasm, ever. You need to make things right for her."

"Yeah, well, thanks but no thanks. That sounds too crazy for me."

But, as often happens in bars, the man drinks a few beers and what used to sound crazy now seems like a real good idea. "Shhwearshh zat pepper tekeela?" he slurs.

First, he grabs hold of the bottle of pepper tequila with both hands and knocks it back in big slurps with tears streaming down his face. Next, he staggers out the back door. And soon all inside hear the most frightful roaring and thumping. Then, silence. The man staggers back into the bar—his shirt's all ripped up and his body has big scratches.

"Now, where'shh zat woman with the sore tooth?"

A Guy Goes Into A Bar

A guy goes into a bar with his dog. Obviously, the bartender doesn't appreciate this and asks him to leave. The man replies, "This is a talking dog." The bartender says, "Yeah, sure, I've heard all about talking dogs . . . now, get out of here!" "No, really," the man says, and he tells the dog to sit at the bar and order some drinks, for he has to get to the men's room fast! So the dog jumps up on the bar stool and the bartender says, "Okay, dog, what will you have?" And the dog says, "Give us two beers, please." The bartender says, "Jesus! You can really talk! How about helping me with something. Take this thirty bucks and go across the street to my friend Bill's bar and play this trick on him." So the dog takes the $30 and splits out the door. Just then the man comes from the bathroom and says, "Where's my dog?" "He went out to do a favor for me, he'll be right back," the bartender explains. *"What do you mean! That's a very specialized and expensive dog, where the hell is he?"* The man flies out of the door, across the street, and stops dead in his tracks as he spots his dog making love to a French poodle on the sidewalk. Confused, the man says, "I never saw you do that before!" and the dog replies, "Well, I never had thirty bucks before!!!"

A Guy Goes Into A Bar

A man's head without a body comes floating into a bar and orders a drink. He sort of slurps the drink down, and all of his torso appears. He orders another drink, slurps that one down, and suddenly he has legs. "This is great," he says to the bartender, "give me another drink. Let's get my arms back." The bartender pours him another, he slurps it down, and suddenly he disappears altogether.

The drunk sitting next to where he was says to the bartender, "He should have quit while he was a head."

A Guy Goes Into A Bar

A guy goes into a bar and is enjoying a drink when a young man with a huge multicolored mohawk takes a seat next to him. He can't help but stare at the young man. "Hey dude, what's your problem?" the mohawked man barks, clearly annoyed. "Didn't you ever do anything crazy when you were young?" "Of course, that's the reason I was staring," replies the older man. "Once when I was young I got really drunk and had sex with a peacock on a dare. I couldn't help wondering if you were my son."

A Guy Goes Into A Bar

A guy goes into a bar and asks for a bottle of forty-year-old Scotch. The bartender, not wanting to go down to the basement and deplete his supply of the rare and expensive liquor, pours a shot of ten-year-old Scotch and figures that his customer won't be able to tell the difference.

The guy downs the Scotch and says, "My good man, that Scotch is only ten years old. I specifically asked for forty-year-old Scotch."

Amazed, the bartender reaches into a locked cabinet underneath the bar and pulls out a bottle of twenty-year-old Scotch and pours the man a shot.

The customer drinks it down and says, "That was twenty-year-old Scotch. I asked for forty-year-old Scotch."

So the bartender goes into the back room and brings out a bottle of thirty-year-old Scotch and pours the customer a drink. By now a small crowd has gathered around the man. Once again, the customer states the true age of the Scotch and repeats his original request for forty-year-old Scotch.

The bartender can hold off no longer and disappears into the cellar and returns with prime, forty-year-old Scotch.

A Guy Goes Into A Bar

The customer downs the Scotch and says, "Now, this is forty-year-old Scotch!"

The crowd applauds his discriminating palate.

An old drunk who has been watching the proceedings with interest raises a full shot glass of his own: "I bet you think you're real smart," slurs the drunk. "Here, take a swig of this."

Rising to the challenge, the guy takes the glass and downs the drink in one swallow. Immediately he chokes and spits out the liquid on the barroom floor.

"My, God!" he exclaims. "That tastes like pee!"

"Great guess," says the drunk. "Now, how old am I?"

A Guy Goes Into A Bar

A guy goes into a bar one afternoon and says to the manager, "I see your sign 'Piano player needed,' and I want you to know I'm your man. Not only that, I write *all* my own material, so you won't ever have to worry about paying royalties to ASCAP or BMI." "Okay," says the manager, "go to the piano and play me a tune." The piano player plays a boogie-woogie that has the manager stomping his feet. "That was great," he says, "What do you call it?" "I call it 'Let Me Kick You in the Butt Until Your Hemorrhoids Bleed!' " says the pianist. "Well," says the manager, "uh . . . that certainly is an unusual name for a song. Let's hear another one."

The piano player plays a haunting melody that brings tears to the manager's eyes it is so beautiful. "What do you call that tune?" asks the manager. "I call it 'Open Your Mouth Wide and Stick Your Tongue Inside Your Nose,' " says the pianist.

The manager replies, "Your playing is great, and I'd like to hire you, but would you be terribly offended if I asked you not to announce the titles of your compositions?" "Not at all," replies the pianist. "You pay, I'll play."

A Guy Goes Into A Bar

That evening the crowd goes wild when the piano player does his first set. When they finally let him take a break, he rushes to the john to relieve himself. On his way out one of the patrons buttonholes him and says, "Wow! You play great!! But tell me, do you know your fly's open and your penis is hanging out?" "Know it? *Hell* . . . I wrote it!"

A Guy Goes Into A Bar

A guy goes into a bar, sits down, and orders a drink. While waiting for the drink to arrive he notices a sailor sitting by himself at the end of the bar. There is something peculiar about this sailor. He is physically normal in every way except that his head is the size of a tangerine. Well, the guy is curious, and after a few more drinks he orders a drink and has the bartender take it to the sailor. When the sailor receives the drink, he looks over at the guy and thanks him. The man sidles up to the sailor and says, "Excuse me, I hope that I'm not being personal, but I can't help but notice that you are physically normal in every way except that your head is the size of a tangerine. If you don't mind me asking, were you born that way or did something happen to you?"

The sailor replies, "Well, it was like this. We were out in the Pacific on maneuvers when the ship sank. I was washed ashore on a desert island. For three months I lived off coconuts and raw fish without any contact with other living beings. One morning I awoke to hear the plaintive cries of a woman in distress. I looked around the island and found a mermaid who was caught on the rocks on the shoreline." The sailor who is physically normal in every way except

A Guy Goes Into A Bar

that his head is the size of a tangerine pauses to sip his drink. Then he continues. "I rescued her and she was so grateful that she offered me three wishes. Having eaten nothing but coconuts and raw fish for three months, I first asked for a steak dinner complete with baked potato and Texas toast. It was great. The mermaid then asked, 'And what is your second wish?' I replied, rather illogically, I must admit, 'Well, for my third wish I'd like to go home. But before that, my second wish . . . well, you see, I've been on this island for three months. It's been over three months since I had sex with a woman.'" The sailor who is physically normal in *every* way except that his head is the size of a tangerine pauses again. "'What I would really like,' I said to the mermaid, 'is to have sex with you.' The mermaid looked at me sadly. 'I would like to accommodate you, but as you can see, from the waist down I am a fish!' I thought for a moment, looked her in the eye, and said, 'Well then, how about a little head?' *Poof!*"

A Guy Goes Into A Bar

An atom goes into a bar. The bartender says, "Why so glum?" The atom says, "I lost my electron." The bartender says, "That's terrible, are you sure?" The atom says, "Yes, I'm positive."

A woman goes into a bar. She is blond, beautiful, buxom, but not too bright. She sits next to her two friends; one is a redhead and the other is a brunette. The bartender asks the redhead what she would like.

She says, "I'll have an A.L." The bartender looks lost and so the redhead says, "Duh, an Amstel Light!"

Next, the bartender asks the brunette what she would like. The brunette says, "I'll have a B.L." With this, the bartender gets a grin on his face and says, "A Bud Light, right?" The brunette says, "Duh, a Beck's Lite!"

Feeling really dumb, he asks the blond what she would like to drink. The blond says, "I'll have a fifteen." The bartender says to himself, "A fifteen, a fifteen, a fifteen?" The blond says, "Duh, a Seven and Seven."

A Guy Goes Into A Bar

A woman goes into a bar carrying a duck under her arm. "Get that pig out of here!" yells the bartender.

"That's not a pig, stupid!" she replies. "That's a duck!"

"I know!" says the bartender. "I was talking to the duck!"

A woman goes into a bar wearing such a tight pair of pants that the lounge lizard watching her asks, "Hey, honey, how do you get into your pants?"

She smiles and says, "Well, you can start by ordering me a drink!"

A Guy Goes Into A Bar

Six men who were feeling no pain staggered out of the bar and headed down the street at about one in the morning. Laughing and singing loudly, they walked up to a two-story home. One of them managed to make it to the door and pounded on the doorbell insistently. A light came on in an upstairs window. The spokesman for the group yelled up, "Is this where Mr. John Smith lives?" "Yes, it is. What do you want?" "Are you Mrs. Smith?" "I am Mrs. Smith. What do you want?" "Could you come down here and pick out Mr. Smith so the rest of us can go home?"

A Guy Goes Into A Bar

A guy goes into a bar. "Pour me a stiff one, Eddie. I just had another fight with the little woman." "Oh, yeah," says Eddie. "And how did this one end?" "When it was over," the guy replies, "she came to me on her hands and knees." "Really? Now that's a switch! What did she say?" "She said, 'Come out from under the bed, you gutless weasel!'"

A Guy Goes Into A Bar

A mouse and a lion go into a bar and they're sitting drinking martinis when a giraffe walks in.

"Get a load of her," says the mouse.

"Well, why not try your luck?" says the lion.

So the mouse goes over to the giraffe and starts talking to her, and within five minutes they're out the door and gone into the night.

The next day, the lion is in the bar drinking away and the mouse staggers in, absolutely exhausted. The lion helps his pal up onto a stool, buys him a drink, and says, "What the hell happened to you? I saw you leave with the giraffe, what happened after that? Was she all right?"

The mouse says, "Yeah, she was really something else—we went out to dinner, had a couple of glasses of wine, and she invited me back to her place to spend the night, and oh, man! I've never had a night like it!" "But how come you look like you're so exhausted?" asks the lion.

"Well," says the mouse, "between the kissing and the hugging I must have run a thousand miles!"

A Guy Goes Into A Bar

A guy goes into a bar and proceeds to get stinking drunk. After a while he sidles up to a girl and, in trying to get her to go home with him, says, "Hey, baby, how do you like your eggs in the morning?" The girl replies, "Unfertilized. Beat it!"

A Guy Goes Into A Bar

A guy goes into a bar to attend a Halloween party. His wife had come down with a terrible headache and had told her husband to go to the bar alone. He, being a devoted husband, protested, but she argued and said she was going to take some aspirin and go to bed, and there was no need of his good time being spoiled by not going. So he took his costume and away he went. The wife, after sleeping soundly for one hour, awakens without pain, and as it is still early, she decides to go to the Halloween party. Inasmuch as her husband does not know what her costume is, she thinks she'll have some fun by watching how her husband acts when she's not with him. She joins the party and soon spots her husband cavorting around on the dance floor, dancing with every woman he can find, and copping a little feel here and a little kiss there. His wife sidles up to him and, since she's a rather seductive babe herself, he leaves his partner high and dry and devotes his time to the new stuff that has just arrived. She lets him go as far as he wishes— naturally, since he's her husband. Finally he whispers a little proposition in her ear and she agrees, so off they go to one of the cars and have a little fun. Just before unmasking at midnight, she slips away and goes home and puts the costume away and gets into bed, wondering what kind of an explanation he'll make for his behavior. She's sitting up reading when he comes in, and she asks what kind of a time he had. He says, "Oh, the same old thing. You know I never have a good time when you're not there." Then she asks, "Did you dance much?" He replies, "I'll tell you, I never even danced one dance. When I got there, I met Pete, Bill Brown, and some other guys, so we went into the back room of the bar and played poker all evening. But I'll tell you . . . the guy I loaned my costume to sure had a real good time!"

A guy goes into a bar on the moon complaining, "The drinks are okay, but there is no atmosphere."

A Guy Goes Into A Bar

A guy goes into a bar and announces, "If anyone can drink twenty pints of Guinness, I will not only pay for it, but I'll give him a hundred dollars." The bartender pours the twenty pints and lines them up at the bar. The man sitting next to him gets up and leaves. He looks around and no one is taking his challenge. The man who left returns to the bar and states proudly that he can drink all twenty pints. So he does. The man is amazed and gives him the money. Then he asks where he went. "Well, I had to go to the bar next door and make sure I could do it first."

A guy goes into a bar and says to the bartender, "Man, I'm dying to have sex in the worst way." So the bartender says, "Well, the worst way I know of is standing up in a hammock."

A Guy Goes Into A Bar

A guy goes into a bar so drunk that he can barely stand up and orders a drink. The bartender says, "No way, buddy, you're too drunk." A few minutes later the drunk comes in through the bathrooms and again slurs, "Give me a drink." The bartender says, "No, man, I told you last time, you're too drunk." Five minutes later the guy comes in through the back door and orders a drink. Again, the bartender says, "You're too drunk." The drunk scratches his head and says, "Damn, I must be. The last two places said the same thing."

So this lawyer goes into a bar and asks, "Is this where I take the exam?"

A Guy Goes Into A Bar

A Californian, a Texan, and a New Yorker go into a seedy bar to enjoy a few drinks. The Californian grabs his wine spritzer, knocks it back in one gulp, and throws the glass against the back wall, smashing it into pieces. He tells the other startled drinkers that the standard of living is so high in California that they never drink out of the same glass twice. Next the Texan finishes drinking his margarita and throws his glass against the back wall. He loudly proclaims that in Texas not only are they all rich from oil, but they have so much sand that glass is cheap, and they too never drink out of the same glass twice. Next the New Yorker drinks his beer, pulls out his Saturday night special, and shoots the Californian and the Texan. As he is putting his gun back in his pants, he tells the wide-eyed bartender that in New York they have so many Texans and Californians that they never have to drink with the same ones twice.

A Guy Goes Into A Bar

A guy goes into a bar and sees the Lone Ranger and Tonto at the bar drinking. The guy yells, "Whose white horse is that outside?" The Lone Ranger finishes off his sarsaparilla, slams down the glass, turns around, and says, "It's my horse. Why do you want to know?" The guy looks at him and says, "Well, your horse is standing out there in the sun and he don't look too good." The Lone Ranger and Tonto run outside and they see that Silver is in bad shape, suffering from heat exhaustion. The Lone Ranger moves his horse into the shade and gets a bucket of water. He then pours some of the water over the horse and gives the rest to Silver to drink. It is then he notices that there isn't a breeze so he asks Tonto if he would start running around Silver to get some air flowing and perhaps cool him down. Being a faithful friend, Tonto starts running around Silver. The Lone Ranger goes back into the bar and orders another drink. A short time later a cowboy walks in and says, "Whose white horse is that outside?" Slowly the Lone Ranger turns around and says, "That is my horse, what is wrong with him now?" "Nothing," replies the cowboy, "I just wanted to let you know that you left your Injun running."

A Guy Goes Into A Bar

A guy goes into a bar to meet his two friends for some serious consumption. His first friend says, "I think my wife is having an affair with the electrician. The other day I came home and found wire cutters under our bed and they weren't mine." His second friend says, "I think my wife is having an affair with the plumber. The other day I found a wrench under the bed and it wasn't mine." Our guy says, "I think my wife is having an affair with a horse." Both his friends look at him with utter disbelief. "No, I'm serious. The other day I came home and found a jockey under our bed."

A Guy Goes Into A Bar

A guy goes into a bar and orders a drink. The bartender delivers his drink and shouts out to the bar patrons, "Forty-six!" Everyone starts to laugh. Next he shouts out, "Thirty-nine!" The patrons laugh even louder. Lastly, he shouts, "Fourteen!" Now people are wiping tears from their eyes from all the laughing. The visitor is curious, so he asks the bartender, "What is going on?" The bartender says, "This is a small town, with small, impressionable children, and so we decided to put numbers to off-color jokes rather than tell them in full." The visitor is astounded. "Let me try!" he says. So he shouts, "Forty-six!" Nothing happens. "Thirty-nine!" Still nothing. "Fourteen!" and yet still not a sound from the patrons. The visitor says to the bartender, "I don't understand. I used exactly the same numbers you did and got a completely opposite response." The bartender replies, "You told it wrong."

A Guy Goes Into A Bar

A guy goes into a bar and proceeds to get stinking drunk. After a few hours of steady drinking the guy leaves and goes out to his car. He is stunned at what he sees. He phones the police to report that thieves have broken into his car. "They've stolen the dashboard, the steering wheel, the brake pedal, even the accelerator," he cries out. However, before the police investigation can start, the phone rings a second time and the same voice comes over the line. "Never mind," he says with a hiccup, "I got in the back seat by mistake."

A cowboy goes into a bar, dressed entirely in paper. Wasn't long before he was arrested for rustling.

A Guy Goes Into A Bar

On New Year's Eve all the wives of the regular patrons of the bar suggested that at the stroke of midnight every husband should stand next to the one person who has made his life worth living. Well, it was kind of embarrassing. The bartender was almost crushed to death.

A guy goes into a bar and sits down on a stool next to a beautiful woman. After a couple of minutes pass he turns to her and asks, "Would you be willing to go to bed with me for a million dollars?" She hesitates for a few seconds and then says, "Yes, for a million dollars I sure would." The man then asks, "Would you go to bed with me for a dollar?" The woman gets angry and says, "Just what kind of a woman do you think I am?" "Well," the man says, "we've already established that. All we are doing now is haggling over the price."

A Guy Goes Into A Bar

A guy goes into a bar after work to have a couple of drinks before catching the ferryboat home. After four martinis he is feeling no pain. When he finally arrives at the ferry slip, the ferryboat is just eight feet from the dock. Afraid of missing this one and being late for dinner, he takes a running leap and lands right on the deck of the boat. "How did you like that jump, buddy?" says the proud guy to a deckhand. "It was great," says the sailor. "But why didn't you wait? We were just pulling in!"

A guy goes into a bar and stays until the bar closes and, no surprise, he is very, very drunk. He leaves, gets on his bus, staggers up the aisle, and sits next to an elderly woman. She looks the man up and down and says, "I've got news for you. You're going straight to hell!" The man jumps up out of his seat and shouts, "Damn, I'm on the wrong bus!"

A Guy Goes Into A Bar

A guy goes into a bar and begins to get seriously loaded and, after staring for some time at the only woman seated at the bar, he walks over to her and takes a firm hold of her left breast. She jumps up and slaps him silly. He immediately apologizes and explains, "I'm sorry. I thought you were my wife. You look exactly like her." "Why you worthless, insufferable, wretched, no-good drunk!" "Funny," he mutters, "you even sound like her."

A rabbi, a priest, and a minister go into a bar. The bartender says, "Hey, what is this, some kind of joke?"

A Guy Goes Into A Bar

A guy goes into a bar and stays about two hours, ordering drink after drink. He then mentions to the bartender something about his girlfriend being out in the car. The bartender, concerned because it's so cold, goes to check on her. When he looks inside the car, he sees the man's buddy, Pete, and his girlfriend going at it in the back seat. The bartender shakes his head and walks back inside. He tells the drunk he thinks it might be a good idea to check on his girlfriend. The fellow staggers outside to the car, sees his buddy and his girlfriend entwined, then walks back into the bar laughing. "What's so funny?" the bartender asks. "That stupid Pete!" the fellow snickers. "He's so drunk, he thinks he's me!"

A Guy Goes Into A Bar

Three vampires walk into a bar and sit down at a table. The waitress comes over and asks the first vampire what he would like. The first vampire responds, "I vould like some blood." The waitress turns to the second vampire and asks what he would like. The vampire responds, "I vould like some blood." The waitress turns to the third vampire and asks what he would like. The vampire responds, "I vould like some plasma." The waitress looks up and says, "Let me see if I have this order correct. You want two bloods and a blood light."

A Guy Goes Into A Bar

A guy goes into a bar and demands the strongest whiskey they have. The bartender, noticing that the man is as angry as hell, pours him a double of Jack Daniel's. The man swills down the drink and says, "Gimme another one." The bartender pours the drink but says, "Now, before I give you this, why don't you let off a little steam and tell me why you're so upset?" "Well, I was sitting in the bar next door when this gorgeous blond slinks in and actually sits beside me at the bar. I thought, 'Wow, this has never happened before.' You know, it was kind of a fantasy come true. Well, a couple of minutes later I feel this hand moving around in my lap and the blond leans over, licks my ear, and asks if I'm interested. I couldn't believe this was happening. I managed to nod my head yes, so she grabbed my hand and we started walking out of the bar. This was just too good to be true." He continues, "She took me down the street to a nice hotel and up to her room. As soon as she shut the door, she slipped out of her dress. That was all she was wearing! I tell you, it didn't take me much longer to get out of my clothes, But, as soon as I jumped into the bed, I heard some keys jingling and someone fumbling with the door. Then she says, 'Oh, my God, it's my boyfriend. He must have lost his wrestling match tonight, he's gonna be real mad. Quick, hide!' So I opened the closet, but I figured that was probably the first place he would look, so I didn't hide there. Then I looked under the bed, but no, I figured he's bound to look there, too. By now, I could hear the key in the lock. I noticed the window was open, so I climbed out and was hanging there by my fingers, praying that the guy wouldn't see me." The bartender says, "Well I can see how you might be scared to death at this point." "Well, yeah, but I hear the guy finally get the door open and he yells out, 'Who you been sleeping with now?' The girl says, 'Nobody, honey, come to bed and calm down.' Well, the guy starts destroying the room. I hear him tear the door off the closet and throw it across the room. I'm thinking, 'Boy, I'm glad I didn't hide in there.' Then he turns over the bed. Good thing I didn't hide under there either. Then I heard him say, 'What's that over there by the window?' I think, 'Oh, God, I'm dead meat now.' But the blond by now is trying real hard to distract him and convince him to stop looking. Well, I hear the guy go into the bathroom and I hear water running for a long time and I figure maybe he's gonna take a bath or something, when all of a sudden, the jerk pours a pitcher of scalding hot water out of the window right on top of my head. I mean, look at this,

A Guy Goes Into A Bar

I got second-degree burns all over my scalp and shoulders!" The bartender says, "Oh man, that would have pissed me off for sure." "No, that didn't really bother me. Next the guy starts slamming the window shut on my hands. I mean, look at my fingers. They're a bloody mess. I can hardly hold on to this glass." The bartender looks at the guy's hands and says, "Yeah, buddy, I can understand why you are so upset." "No, that wasn't what really got me crazy." The bartender then asks in exasperation, "Well, then, what did finally get you angry?" "Well, as I was hanging there I finally got the courage to turn around and look down and I was only about six inches off the ground."

So a dyslexic walks into a bra . . .

A Guy Goes Into A Bar

A guy goes into a bar, sits down, and begins to drink very slowly. On his face is the saddest hangdog expression. The bartender asks, "What's the matter? Are you having troubles with your wife again?" The man says, "Yes, we did have a fight and she told me that she wasn't going to speak to me for a month." The bartender says, "That should make you happy." The man sadly shoots his head up and says, "No, the month is up today!"

A guy goes into a bar one evening sporting a matched pair of swollen black eyes that look extremely painful. "Whoa!" says the bartender. "Who gave those beauties to you?" "Nobody gave them to me," says the guy, "I had to fight like crazy for both of them."

A Guy Goes Into A Bar

There was a big conference of beer producers in Amsterdam, in the Netherlands. At the end of the day the presidents of all the beer companies decided to have a drink at the bar. The president of Budweiser ordered a Bud, the president of Carlsberg ordered a Carlsberg, and the list went on. . . . Then the waitress asked Freddie Heineken what he wanted to drink, and much to everyone's amazement, Mr. Heineken ordered a Coke! "Why don't you order a Heineken?" his colleagues asked. "Naah. If you guys won't drink beer, then neither will I."

A Guy Goes Into A Bar

A guy goes into a bar with a parrot on his shoulder. The guy is a black man from Nigeria and is wearing the colorful ceremonial garb of his native land. The bartender says, "What an exquisite creature! Where did you get it?" "Africa," replies the parrot.

A Frenchman, an Italian, and an American were sitting in a bar discussing sex. "Last night I made love to my wife three times," boasted the Frenchman. "She was in sheer ecstasy this morning." The Italian said, "Ah, last night I made love to my wife six times, and this morning she made me a wonderful omelet and told me she could never love another man." When the American remained silent, the Frenchman smugly asked, "And how many times did you make love to your wife last night?" "Once," he replied. "Only once?" the Italian arrogantly snorted. "And what did she say to you this morning?" he asked. "Don't stop."

A Guy Goes Into A Bar

A guy goes into a bar and orders a triple Scotch whiskey. The bartender pours him the drink and says, "That's quite a heavy drink. What's wrong?" After downing his drink, the guy says, "I got home and found my wife in bed with my best friend." "Wow," says the bartender. "No wonder you needed a stiff drink. The second triple is on the house." As the man downs his second triple Scotch, the bartender asks him, "What did you do?" The guy says, "I walked over to my wife, looked her straight in the eye, and told her that we were through and to get the hell out." The bartender says, "That makes sense, but what about your best friend?" The guy says, "I walked over to him, looked him right in the eye, and said, '*Bad dog!*'"

A Guy Goes Into A Bar

A guy goes into a bar, and after downing only one drink he starts to cry. The bartender approaches him and asks what's wrong. The guy answers, "I'm eighty-seven years old and I just got married to a twenty-five-year-old woman." The bartender nods his head, saying, "Don't worry, it may seem that you don't have a lot in common, but maybe this is an opportunity for each of you to grow." The old man shakes his head, saying, "No, that's not the problem! We have everything in common! She's smart, funny, and wonderful to be around." The bartender looks at the man, confused, then says, "So you're worried she just married you for your money then?" The old man says, "No, she's an heiress. She has twice the money I do." The bartender is even more confused now. "Is it a sex problem? I know a great urologist." The old man shakes his head and howls, "No, no. We make love morning, noon, and night." The bartender gives him a look of bewilderment and says, "It sounds like you have the perfect relationship. Why are you crying?" The old man answers, "I can't remember where I live!!!"

A Guy Goes Into A Bar

A grasshopper goes into a bar and orders a beer. The bartender says, "You know, we have a drink named after you here."

The grasshopper looks puzzled and replies, "You have a drink named Fred?"

An Englishman, a Frenchman, and a Polish man are sitting in a bar drinking and discussing how stupid their wives are. The Englishman says, "I tell you, my wife is so stupid that last week she went to the supermarket and bought $300 worth of meat because it was on sale, and we don't even have a fridge to keep it in." The Frenchman agrees, but says his wife is even stupider. "Just last week she went out and spent $17,000 on a new car," he laments, "and she doesn't even know how to drive!" But the Pole still thinks his wife is dumber. "Ah, it kills me every time I think of it," he chuckles. "My wife left to go on a trip to Greece. I watched her packing her bag and she must have put a hundred condoms in there, and she doesn't even have a penis!"

A Guy Goes Into A Bar

Descartes walks into a bar and the bartender asks, "Would you like a beer?" Descartes replies, "I think not," and *poof*—he vanishes.

A guy goes into a bar wearing a stovepipe hat, a waistcoat, and a beard, sits down at the bar, and orders a drink. As the bartender sets it down he asks, "Are you going to a costume party?" "Yeah," the man answers, "I'm supposed to come dressed as my love life." "But you look like Abe Lincoln," protests the bartender. "That's right. My last four scores were seven years ago."

A Guy Goes Into A Bar

A cowboy goes into a bar after riding his horse into a new town. Unfortunately, the locals have a habit of picking on strangers, which he was. When he finishes his drink he finds that his horse has been stolen. He goes back into the bar, handily flips his gun into the air, catches it above his head without even looking, and fires a shot into the ceiling. "Which one of you sidewinders stole my hoss?" he yells with surprising forcefulness. No one answers. "All right, I'm gonna have another beer, and if my hoss ain't back outside by the time I finish, I'm gonna do what I done in Texas! And I don't like to have to do what I done in Texas!" Some of the locals shift restlessly. He has another beer, walks outside, and his horse is back! He saddles up and starts to ride out of town. The bartender wanders out of the bar and asks, "Say, partner, before you go . . . what did you do in Texas?" The cowboy turns back and says, "I had to walk home."

A Guy Goes Into A Bar

A guy goes into a bar and sees a friend at a table drinking by himself. Approaching the friend he comments, "You look terrible, what's the problem?" "My mother died in June," he says, "and left me $10,000." "Gee, that's tough," he replies. "Then in July," the friend continues, "my father died, leaving me $50,000." "Wow, two parents gone in two months, no wonder you're depressed." "And last month my aunt died and left me $15,000." "Three close family members lost in three months? How sad." "Then this month," continues the friend, "nothing!"

A Guy Goes Into A Bar

A guy goes into a bar at four o'clock in the afternoon and begins to drink. It gets to be ten p.m. and he is about ready to go home when the bartender says to him, "Hey, Ralph, why are you going home so soon? I usually see you here until way past midnight. Something wrong?" The guy responds, "No, nothing wrong, just got a sore behind from sitting on this stool for so long." "Ralph, I got just the thing for you," says the bartender as he reaches up to the top shelf behind the bar. He grabs a bottle of pills, opens the bottle, and hands Ralph two pills. Ralph says "What are these, aspirin?" "No," says the bartender. "Stool softener."

A Guy Goes Into A Bar

A guy goes into a bar one winter night in Alaska during a severe blizzard. The temperature is forty below zero and dropping. Since he's a steady customer, he never reaches into his pocket to pay. The bartender says, "You owe me quite a bit on your tab." "Sorry," says the guy. "I'm flat broke this week." "That's okay," says the bartender. "I'll just write your name and the amount you owe me right here on the wall." "But," says the guy, "I don't want any of my friends to see that; they'll think I'm a deadbeat." "No they won't," says the bartender. 'I'll just hang your parka over it until it's paid."

A guy goes into a bar that he had frequented daily for the last sixty years. It was his ninetieth birthday so the bartender and his friends decided to surprise him. They wheeled in a big birthday cake and out popped a beautiful young woman who said, "Hi, I can give you some super sex!" And the old man said, "Well, I guess I'll take the soup."

A Guy Goes Into A Bar

A guy goes into a bar carrying his tiny toy poodle. The bartender stops him immediately and tells him that no dogs are allowed inside. "I would really like to bring my dog in with me. He is well-groomed, very well-behaved, and he won't create any problems." The bartender, who saw how earnest the man was and how much he appeared to love his dog said, "You know, I've been behind this bar for many years. In all that time I've never had a dog steal glasses, napkins, table covers, or pictures off the wall. I've never had to evict a dog for being drunk and disorderly. And I've never had a dog run out on the bill. Yes, indeed, your dog is welcome to come in. And if your dog is willing to vouch for you, you're welcome to come in, too."